SOME DARK FAMILIAR

SOME DARK FAMILIAR

POEMS

Julia C. Alter

GREEN WRITERS PRESS   *Brattleboro, Vermont*

Printed in the United States

10 9 8 7 6 5 4 3 2 1

Green Writers Press is a Vermont-based publisher whose
mission is to spread a message of hope and renewal through
the words and images we publish. Throughout we will adhere
to our commitment to preserving and protecting the natural
resources of the earth. To that end, a percentage of our proceeds
will be donated to environmental activist groups. Green Writers
Press gratefully acknowledges support from individual donors,
friends, and readers to help support the environment and our
publishing initiative.

Giving Voice to Writers & Artists Who Will Make the World a Better Place
Green Writers Press | Brattleboro, Vermont
www.greenwriterspress.com

sundog
POETRY
Sundog Poetry
www.sundogpoetry.org

ISBN: 979-8-9891784-9-0

PRINTED ON 100% PCW RECYCLED PAPER BY BOOKMOBILE.
BASED IN MINNEAPOLIS, MINNESOTA, BOOKMOBILE BEGAN AS A DESIGN AND TYPESETTING
PRODUCTION HOUSE IN 1982, AND STARTED OFFERING PRINT SERVICES IN 1996.
BOOKMOBILE IS RUN ON 100% WIND- AND SOLAR-POWERED CLEAN ENERGY.

Out in the woods she navigates fine by the moon
but get her around a lightbulb and she's doomed

—Ani DiFranco, "Evolve"

Contents

I. ❧ THE UN-DRINKING

II. ∿ BELLY THE WOLF

III. ∿ OUTSIDE VOICE

I.

THE UN-DRINKING

Who Makes Milk?

Cows, I want to say. But I say
mammas, I say *mammals.*
Whales, even. Milk is made
by a wound, or that's how
I made it for you—the un-making,
the un-drinking. The blue empty, blue
translucent. Sucked teats make it.
Beasts make it. Other mothers.
Better mothers. Udders. Plastic
wheezing suction cups. Hands pulling
down, hands stirring yellow powder
into water. Factories. Flowers.
Women who weep in the shower,
rolling their last pearls down the drain.
Thunder. Hunger. Your mouth,
some whisper in your saliva.
A harder mouth, a darker whisper.
Lips pulling, teeth. Prayers.
Trees. Breathing things.
Nipples that will never heal.

To Alanis Morissette, After Reading About Her Postpartum Depression in My Therapist's Waiting Room

You'll rescue me, right?

I've replaced water
with iced coffee. I only sweat
when I sleep. Nothing happens
in my dreams. I am dead
weight in that specific sea,
that shifty gray gnawing. Your hair
is platinum now, Alanis, but I see
your roots. I know how
we become unrecognizable.
I wore a black maxi dress
with grotesque flowers all summer
so I wouldn't come looking for myself.

They put you on a beach in that blue
and white muumuu, strategically
positioned your kids in front
of your belly, juxtaposed it
with a picture of you ten years ago,
maybe twenty, in a white tank top, wild hair
waving onstage. They want your confession
but not your flesh. They would rather have you
in a muumuu, only your forearms
exposed. Wrists taut from lifting
the baby. They can't see the carpal tunnel

from nursing, the nerve damage
from gripping the toilet seat
in the ugliest waves of labor.

You'll complete me, right?

I know the velvet curtain of sleep
that drops, and the darker curtain behind it.
Alanis, I know the panic
of sensing the baby stirring
out of his nap, what it is to click him
back into his car seat for the third time
in a single afternoon, to ride around
the block again so he will just keep
sleeping. I know the mornings
of pretending I can't hear him
crying so I can keep scrolling
through my phone.

Our thoughts swell
with the commonest of terrors:
the tub   the candles   the stairs
inevitable and relentless as the night
we collapse into. I know that in carrying
our babies we carry the proximity
to death. A mother is forever
an alert and guarded animal,
prowling a forest floor,
one footstep away from a trip
wire into annihilation.

They want even you to be presentable, you
who showed us how to thrash, to throw
our voices like litter out car windows,
yelling *the cross-eyed bear that you gave to me*
when the lyric you wrote was *the cross I bear*.
Now I know what it is to leave
something behind, to wind up
with a misshapen, unwieldy inheritance.
Now I sit in this body of the mother:
part straitjacket, part hot air balloon.

I'll be happy, right?

Alanis, why do they expect us to return
so quickly? Didn't we almost vanish
somewhere back there? Sucked
into the storms of our anatomy,
hammered into the earth.
A surge, we called it, turned inside out,
shattered   shucked   shattered.
They want us to find our old bodies again,
like lost keys, only a few places
they could possibly be.

I'll be worthy, right?

Did you also practice
smiling in the mirror
before inviting them in
to *see the baby?*

When I meet the eyes
of other mothers
in the same mud
I want to say
I love you. I'm sorry.
There's a prayer from a balmy place
that goes like that.

I reach and reach
for a familiar breeze
to part the sea   to coax me
out of my own front door
sunshine   tomato vines
my utter tundra   of summer

another day I do not want
to hold him
only myself

Non-Monogamy (Ether)

Explain it as a conduit
—for an element

awakened in your body—
the space between the space

Neither sedative
nor euphoria

Find another rhyme
for sleep, or another way
to say *sleep over*

My phone notifies me of nothing,
an aperture to the sky

Looking for my plus one
and one
and one . . .

I look for water moving
against water, warming
itself, then becoming air

the way words do

L'Oeuf Chaud Froid

I've said I remember nothing
of the first three months.
But when I start peeling back
the bleary out-of-body shroud,
the stitches, the sitz baths,
there's always the milkstained blue
couch where I would wake in the blue
light, turning off my alarm, turning
on the yellow pump and the TV,
every three hours another automatic
emptying. An ounce or two, less than
half of what you needed. I watched
the California chef pipe Meyer lemon
crème fraîche into an empty egg shell.
The next morning I took scissors
to my head, wet hair punctuating
the floor. I read it like tea leaves:
no room for pretty here.

Milk extracted from my tits
like lemon juice in the eye,
like a man fighting
the urge to cry. Thin cord
of milk pulled reluctantly
from the new abyss
where your body used
to be, a rough white rope
up through my
breast is best.

I'll never forget the sucking
of the machine when you couldn't.
I'd grind my teeth
like I was coming down
off ecstasy when the only thing left
was chills, the useless hollows
of a body shitting and shivering,
feverish and frigid and fragile
as 4 AM,
as baby,
an egg shell
opened up
and ready
to be filled.

Opening Track for Sertraline

O make me a vessel, make me
more boat on ocean than hollow
container. Contain the thunder-
gray ocean. Make me more ocean
than shipwreck. Wreck me less.

Oblong green, stop my blood-
stream from emptying
the glitter out of my brain,
like so many mornings after
the rave is over. The rage is over—
sticky dizziness, an eye's
bewitched twitching.

O make the ache
stop snaking through
my bleak thoughts and I
swear I will bow down
to every earthworm, and finally
learn the names of the flowers.

Revelations

When I burn a photo of myself
in too-pale makeup, graceful
red-nailed fingers laced
around the long neck of a bong

When the baby comes I am purple
butterfly wings, pinned

When I burn a letter to my maiden
self and give the girl who would slink
into cars with strange men to the fire

When the *linea nigra* recedes
and my belly is bone
white again

When I dance and don't think
about the baby for two hours and it feels
like fireworks—not blowing
something into oblivion,
but making a darkness
sharpen and pulse

When I learn that fireworks were invented
in medieval times to ward off evil spirits

When thoughts about the baby are evil spirits

When thoughts about the baby light the whole sky—

a love like that
When I give him the first blowjob since the baby
that isn't for him, but for me—*a love like that*

When I feel my mother's colon
cancer already a phantom bee
buzzing in my gut

When I step away from the mirror
to see myself more clearly, my breath
no longer smudging up the glass

When I can't get my mother to quit
buying stuff for the baby
When my mother becomes a mirror

When she tells me at twelve years old
you don't have the body for short skirts,
and I don't put one on again until this morning

When my therapist asks, *does your mother love you*
unconditionally? and I say *of course, but* . . .

When my mother becomes clear glass
I look through

When my mother becomes clear glass
I shatter

The Basket

On a condom company's website, a photo
of a basket holds two fluffy, newborn bunnies.

A reasonably handsome bearded guy raises
an eyebrow, slightly smirking for the camera to say:

Whoops! Babies. There's a trademark
on Momentum™. I'm tired of irony.

What was I expecting? The condom website winks:
with the right barrier, anything can be avoided.

We ordered a small box of them months ago.
First with high hopes for your birthday,

then our anniversary. When that came
and went we carried the box

in the glove compartment to Florida
for fun nights in the festival tent.

Now the unopened box is a fixture—
a lamp that never gets turned on—on my side of the bed.

When I lie down at night, my mind buzzes
over the tiny body that came out of me.

We can't find a way back to the river
we used to know so well. When you are snoring,

I put my hand between my legs and find
I am still woven shut.

Old Nipple

A long time ago, I found an old nipple
Creatures drink and die at the breast, behind it

       Behind the drinking, a creature is dying
       I die small, splashing an angel on the floor

An angel is a splash of gold on the floor
Translucent milk, pearl water, memory

       A pearl of milk is a memory
       My nipples—puckered up like raspberries

Nipples, puckered and hard, early raspberries.
Can I forget the name of my blood?

       A prayer to bleed and forget these names, the sun.
       Nothing of my body left to feed him,

I left my body to feed him nothing
but a spell. An old nipple, a short time.

The Excavator

I am climbing a hill
holding hands with a man
who isn't my son's father. Tonight,
the moon is a wrecking ball.
Cresting, I see the big machine
bathed in silver light. Stars float
like dust motes swirling in a black window
of sky. A strange construction site.
We find ourselves here, without
any scaffolding, on a hill in a town
far from my baby,
who would be saying
Arm! Boom! Bucket!
Who would be saying
Scoop it! Lift it! Dump it out!
Who would be saying
More work!
Tomorrow I'll be back home
with him and his dad, pushing
his stroller up another hill to watch
workers on Church Street, hobbling
over asphalt that's been hacked up
and crumbled for months.
Neon safety vests, different sweat,
and different cigarettes. Here,
in this freshly shifted earth,
there's a new hole.

Non-Monogamy (Lepidoptera)

Just because moths don't die when we touch
their wings, doesn't mean that we should

The iridescent powder
is made of tiny scales

Not fish nor bird

but the way the word ecstatic also holds static

I was almost ready to swipe it
on my eyelids

Presumptuous
to think that shadow more

than something sent flying
with the edge of a blade

Does it float?
Does it cling?

It's just another kind of dust

Split Lip

From the kitchen, I startle
at his alarming scream—
I run in to see his top lip so swollen
already I can barely get under it.
I test for wiggles with his blood
threading down my finger.
Then I rock and squeeze,
shush and snuggle and hum.
Then a popsicle and *Sesame Street*
while I scrub the smears
from the shiny tiles.

An hour later he's napping, wrapped
in blankets, surrounded by plush.
My son was running in socks
while I was daydreaming
about a lover. Only then, my own tears.
When I lift a hand to clear them,
my son's dried blood on my sleeve
wets again, and darkens.

Mommies

Mommies aren't supposed to be on fire
or fall down a rabbit hole, waving goodbye.

> Like rabbits. Falling. The hole that waves goodbye
> is a kaleidoscope, spinning in fingers.

Fingers twist inside, kaleidoscopic.
A flower spirals toward the center, in flames.

> The center is her self—a flame, a flower,
> she forgets she is also a mother.

Letting herself forget she's a mother,
she descends, the whole planet bottoming,

> the beat drop at the bottom of the world.
> Third eye bloom through sparkling indigo,

third eye spark, sweet dark hello. Bloom & bloom &
Mommies aren't supposed to be on fire

Some Idea

Being in love with some idea of you,
every morning I drink some idea
of coffee on my porch and wonder
if you're awake yet, smoking
your first idea of a cigarette.
Some idea of us sits on a bench
by a river in some idea of Missouri
reading poetry to some idea of each other.
We watch some idea of a bird bring
some idea of a worm to her nestlings.
Some idea of me fucks some idea
of my partner and imagines
your silky electric forearms when I come.
Some idea of me pulls over and weeps
while another idea of me changes
lanes and keeps driving. Some idea of me
needs a thousand miles between us,
and some idea of me needs you.
I want to hook some idea of my thumb
into some idea of your pocket and walk
all the way to some idea of the highway
in the dark with no idea of turning back.
Though some idea of me is a moth,
another idea of me is a mother.
I'm here holding some idea of my son
snuggled in some idea of his dinosaur
blanket, reading his favorite book,
What Do You Do with an Idea?
We recite the last line together:
you change the world . . . we know it
by heart, or by some idea of our hearts.

Pachira aquatica

These days I can live with almost
no light or water

like the Malabar chestnut
I got at IKEA in Philly in 2012,

still here.

So many times I almost let it die, before finding
a yellowed leaf on the floor, how I had to
nearly kill it to remember I was keeping it alive.

A giant jungle tree ends up stunted,
trunk braided, sold for 6.99.

I have to live with it—
the way it lives with me—
never knowing
if water's coming.

Twisties

It's a skeptical ostrich, looking down at a snake
rising from its coil to pray, looking up at a giraffe
giving bad advice. Behind them, two humans dancing.
Having arrived at this moment in this body, this is what I see.
Having arrived at Silk City on a Saturday night in 2013,
I see a man who wants to dance like me, down in the animal
dirt of our bodies, coiling around each other, sampling
our new sweat & gleam. The whole city silking away.
You can't believe it now, when I tell you your dad and I
met on a dance floor. *My daddy doesn't dance!*
you giggle, quizzical. It doesn't feel true, but it is.
Two humans dancing, sharing nothing but the future
fact of you. I could say *went home together,*
but it wasn't that. *Left together. Just left.*

II.

BELLY THE WOLF

Some Dark Familiar

*In outer space, I threw a banana
into the air.* It landed on a planet
of dinosaurs. You know all of them
died, the way you say you'll *die*
your lip by pulling the dry patch
off until it bleeds. Every month
you must think I'm dying,
my panties bloodstained as we sit
on our separate toilets, together.
In outer space, we throw flowers
at the feet of mothers, sent up there
in their raging labors to claim us.
Down here, I have you watch my mouth
for the proper pronunciation, our lips
together unfurling *vagina.*
When you're with your father,
I'm with a lover, stretching out
the syllables of baboons, a babbling
windfall of blessings. I soak the sheets
and meet my only known ancestors,
their liquid skies, born inside
some dark familiar fur.

Yesenia

My son comes home from a weekend
at his dad's, saying, *Yesenia told me*
don't bang my spoon on my plate.
I read Goodnight Moon *with Yesenia*
& Yesenia gave me hugs.

When I show up at his new apartment,
my ex is in bed with Yesenia & I call
up the stairs, *Is anyone home?*

He stumbles out with glitter
on his cheek to show me
our son's room—the bag
of Goodwill clothes, used
stuffed animals, glow-in-the-dark stars
scattered across the ceiling.

Gorgeous in the doorway,
Yesenia reaches out her hand. I shake,
& make myself disappear.

Home alone without
my son, my tongue
shapes her name—
over & over & over.
A terrifying flower,
no one's mother.

The Heart

I want to be Mary when I grow up—
Mary who works the register at Healthy Living.
Mary wants a puppy and braids her long gray hair
and finds everyone forgivable. I'm buying myself flowers
and chocolate, and she's asking me what I'm up to today.
Writing poems, I tell her. *I bet they're straight from the heart*,
she says, ringing me up. Driving home, my mind sparks
to the teacher who told me: *never put love, tears, or heart
    in a poem.*
Sparks then to the cow's heart—the literal heart of a cow—
that my ex brought to a PEX Valentine's party in Philly
two decades ago. My heart was ancient then.
Watching clusters of burners on molly & acid peek
at this disembodied piece of beef, this bloody mass
in a plastic bin. I went outside and puked in an alley.
He carried it around all night, feeling clever.
He didn't put it on ice. He must have thrown it out
before the sun came up. I know no one
ate or buried it. We couldn't give it back.
That cow died once, then died again,
thumped in a trash can, under the stars.

Non-Monogamy (Bad Reasons)

When I say I love you,
you say covered in wings,
or covered in wind
A band name or a catalogue
of alibis   The Most Private Thing
is an alien   a tent
of hair   a mushroom
And a mushroom
is a big white shaggy heart
multiplying in the dark
without blood   without seed
A mirror of owls
a scale of fish   our sacred geometry
and the sounds
we make on snow

When a Bird Gets Trapped in Your House

Your son is on your lap, biting
the heads off cheddar bunnies.
You send a silent prayer to the god
of children and winged things
that his dad's girlfriend picks him up
for the weekend before the bird
gets really frenzied, chittering and shitting,
her anxiety gathering bile up into your throat.
You don't ask your neighbor Mr. Irby what to do
about the bird freaking out in your house
because you don't want to remind him
you're a woman living alone with her son,
or on other days just living completely
alone, or feel your shame at knowing nothing
about how to free a trapped thing,
or feel your shame at building a house
with a window no one can reach, not even
with a ladder. Shame for not having a ladder,
and shame for having a window
only a bird can reach, believing it's her way
back to the sky and if she bangs so hard she forgets
her body she'll get there. You watch her slam
her tiny body into that window for an entire afternoon.
You chug wine and walk in circles and google
how to free trapped birds. The way they say to do it
is with another person and a sheet, but you can't
reach anyone, and you can't reach her. So you open
the screen doors and leave a light on the porch
and the bowl of birdseed your son put out before he left

for the weekend, thinking maybe she's like a dog
and would follow the scent of the seed.
You get in your car and drive to a musty apartment,
get under the sheets, slam your body into something
and hope it gets you free.

Non-Monogamy (Bumble)

The swipe is a wing,
a yellow-headed match.
It starts with sleepless,
the obvious honey.
The hive, the kingdom
of plurality, the radiant
bloom of family.

The flower's head takes nothing
from the petals, and the petals
take nothing but a bow
in the breeze.

Your name is husked
in the buzzword of your love.
Take their stingers out,
and now the bees just sing.

Sweet Child O' Mine

It's 5 AM on Friday and I've let the dog out,
climbed back into bed with my son,
who snores splayed out with his little hand
down his PJ pants like a little man,
the one he's expected to be when he leaves
for his dad's every weekend.

They play video games, drink soda,
watch PG-13 movies. The endless talk
of battles, of shooting. He reports back
to me through strange behaviors.
Last week, kissing me deep and hard
on the mouth with his hands in my hair
because *Catwoman kisses like that.*
Recognizing every brand name snack
at the drugstore, imploring me
for Hot Cheetos, Lucky Charms, Sour Patch Kids.

I joke to friends, calling it his Second Life.
On weekends we're avatars, moving through
each other's imaginary worlds. He goes
to music festivals, sleeps on stranger's couches,
wears backwards baseball caps, never takes a nap.
I go to Canada because he knows I went there
once before, crossed a border into another land.

I like that song from Thor: Love and Thunder—
Sweet Child Alive—he announces on a drive.
And now we're listening to Guns N' Roses.

Sunday nights I take him back in.
He smells like roses,
like thunder,
like a love I know
could kill me, and the linger
of sunscreen that didn't wash off in the bath.

He's alive—and he belongs to no one.

Only the Snow

I can't be   more than my one body
if I'm not   my one body first

I can't be

              more   than my body

Remember—no one can come in with you
Remember the roof's   gray

It will feel electric   wrapping nerves
      in numbness

The shock   will shine   like a bad diamond

Like a light   contraction,
      but taking something away

Outside, a single crow   will scour the snow
      for silver

Tonight, only the snow can hold me

I said no   to a new life   it was easy—
          barely anything there.

Colorado

If you don't want a baby, you'll have to call the moon.

I spent my life as the soft-tapping hermit crab,

a creature imprinting the squiggled line

between land and water. Or I spent my life

as the flirtatious snail, occupying a thigh.

A reminder to come from round things,

from squish and from circles. From the pulsing

middles of whole shells. I came from slimy openings.

I count up every petal and find my own

mathematical flower, the part of me that wants

numbers, existing shapes, correct things.

To slink all the way back through that

divine portal. What's the opposite of a mother?

Non-Monogamy (Sunflower)

If you let your hair loose and become a sunflower.
If you find the perfect filter for the stars, a device,
a dial. If we find a way to comprehend the pupil
of an echinacea, or how we came to be standing
here, with a blowtorch, trying to ignite
a damp pile of leaves. If swirling ash
becomes the flit of a bat. Or a hand is a crotch,
but also a whole body. If a shooting star
is made out of titanium. If we hear an EDM cover
of "Walking in Memphis" while pulling
our clothes down to black. If you say,
I want you like that
or you say she sent you a hat.
If you live at the top of that hobbling,
no one can reach you all winter.
If you pull frozen pizzas through the woods on a sled.
Or the center of the center is red.
If it makes you feel small, or like anything
is possible, or nothing. If wool socks in August.
If the tickling story leaves me speechless.
If you're alone in the MOMA.
If you're kneeling behind me on the bed
and I lower my face into blackberries—

Swan

It's her actual name.
I'm dancing alone and it isn't a metaphor.
My body in the window, my body's blue movement
in the blue vervain reflected in the window.
I don't know how to make the tinctures I need
from these wildflowers in my own back yard.
When the beat drops, moths rise around me.
I'm not saying I'm luminous, just that
I have a cigarette in my mouth.
Tonight I am the queen of peaches.
Tonight I am the queen of eating
my own words, of drinking
my own medicine. I move from wine
to gin. I wanted other women
to love you so I didn't have to watch you
die. Now you have a woman riding
on the back of your bike, wearing
the helmet that made my back hurt
because my neck is almost too long
& narrow to hold my head
up. You tell me we're *so similar*—
me and this strange woman,
this spooky bird that mates for life.

Spilanthes americana

He brings home a packet
in his pocket, printed
with roots and trees.
His dad's girlfriend sent it,
knowing I know nothing
about seeds, that I'd need her
help to plant them properly.
Annual? Perennial?
She showed up,
and she can leave.
She laughs at me for keeping him
a baby. I know what she sees—
that I still wipe his butt,
that he still sleeps with me.
Everything's dying, so why wouldn't he?
Maplefields where sugar maples used to be.
He says, *I want to live under a tree*
and all the seeds spill out of me.
Oh say can you see—my son,
my anthem, my bunny-bee—

Rutland

At Christmas, my sister asks *do you ever think about it?*
Never, I say, shocking myself at the quick and simple
    truth.
She says, *I just feel like a baby is always a good thing.*
And I say, *that wasn't a baby, though.*

It was a ghost passing through me.

The memory comes back jarring, blazing
sunlight on a single-digit day. I'm driving south
to a cabin in the woods for a retreat
because my son is with his father,
and because I don't have a baby.

The gray building is still there, between
a Little Caesars Pizza and a church
with a letterboard:
be kind whenever possible.

I try to model kindness for my son,
who goes on hitting me and screaming
that he hates me while I try to love
the ways he stumbles over being human.

I traveled two hours because no provider
in town had openings. I was already sick
in that particular way, my breasts
speaking a heavy urgent language.

The nurse was kind. She held my hand
because no one was allowed in the room with me,
because all around us, humans were dying
from a strange disease. So I squeezed a stranger's hand,
a kind stranger, a soft woman who gave me
Teddy Grahams and apple juice
when I almost fainted from the strangeness of it all.

I think of my friend who needed a year
of therapy after having an emergency
C-section instead of a "natural birth." I think of
Little Caesars Pizza, how C-sections were also named
after the emperor, or after the Latin word "caedere,"
meaning "to cut." I think of the rolling blade
of a pizza cutter, and I think about the ways that
babies try to tell our bodies they're not ready
for this particular world.

Yesterday over bowls of cereal at our kitchen counter
my kid asked, *do you ever feel lonely, Mommy?*

My troubled angel, my brotherless son.

Uvalde

I'm American, in my comfortable sadness,
ruminating over backyard deer. My American
sadness, I wear it like my ayahuasca necklace.
It used to mean something. Now it hangs around
my throat, hand-beaded in a wet dark forest
where I was once a human. Today I'm tired
of gratitude—even tired of trees, with trees
surrounding me—the audacity. I see them in relief,
in the darkness where they part. Just swallow me.
When you look up the leaves are so sparkly, my son says,
looking up. Beyond the wildest drug trip,
the things our kids might say, what they might do,
and what could happen to them. Trees in Texas,
Texas ash. Nineteen mothers' children.

Roden Crater

Roden Crater is a gateway to observe light, time and space

When I saw the models—ceramic, metallic, phallic—I
    was doing that thing where I walk
through a museum pretending to feel something, which
    is a feeling close to the feeling of
acquiring an extinct volcano, which this man did, so he
    could make something visible from space.

I wander through the exhibit, nodding dumbly, then
    check out the strobe light installation
that feels the same whether I close my eyes or open
    them—which is curious, when talking
about light. I can't tell what's behind my eyelids or in
    front of them, but the guy with the
orange beanie perched on his head keeps making loud
    sounds so he can hear his voice echo
through this sterile box of light. He's starting to annoy
    me, and we're all wearing disposable
blue shoe covers over our boots.

//

I go back to the cabin and google Roden Crater, after
    smoking a little weed and heading out
for a snowshoe on Owl Path to the edge of a cliff,
    finding the mushrooms like so many moth
wings up and down the birch. They mingle with the
    bark, they baffle the wind. The snow is

like superfine sugar, dissolving quicker in the type of
    sunlight that makes you want to be the
highest leaf on the tree. Some black-capped chickadees
    are having a whole conversation.

//

I swear the bird's eye view of Roden Crater looks just
    like one of those moth-wing mushrooms.

Google says it might be finished by 2024, with a
    10-million-dollar investment from Kanye West.

//

I text a friend, a mushroom lover—
What are those lil guys called?
The ones that look like marbled wing-y things?

Now I know they're called Turkey Tails,
and I don't want to live in a world without them.

Aubrie Sends a Voice Memo from the Salton Sea

We're drinking a beer together,
three thousand miles apart.
It's Saturday. The sun's a little spooky.
Sometimes my heart is California.
So many orange groves. Greed.
Wine country.
Fish bones in a desert.
Rushed for nuggets of gold.
Filled with famous people.
The way it squeezes
everything for water—

Reddit

I'm buying him the eight dollar bath bomb
because he got two shots in his arm and screamed
I feel like I'm dying, mommy!
as I held his elbows down. He loves the fizz
and tingle on his skin, how he never knows
what kind of creature is hiding in there
when it all dissolves.

The woman at the fancy gift shop lets us know
her bunny's name is the same as my son's.
I tell her I call my son my bunny, but don't tell her
I call my asshole my bunny hole, and that I show
my bunny hole to strangers on the internet for money
I don't need. Strangers in their mother's basements,
strangers married to MILFs they've stopped fucking.
Strangers with dead mothers, mothers on drugs,
and mothers who never hugged them. Strangers
who call me *babygirl*, and strangers who call me *mommy*.

There's a coyote in the field tonight
that may have rabies, or else has lost
its mother. It just keeps circling—
looking back at me.

III. ∾

OUTSIDE VOICE

I'm Supposed to be Writing a Nature Poem

I came here to listen to the trees,
to rifle through my apologies.

The stream is either shimmering
or shivering, like someone's shaking

a glass jar full of glass shards at the sun.
Do I eat the moss, or just put my face in it?

This morning my son pronounced *rifle* as *riffle*
when cocking his imaginary gun.

Stone Fruit

We would have been heckled
by the sun. Stippled, dripped
& dappled. First date soulmates.
All your birds would have come
undone, every bird call in North America.
Goldfinch of your voice memos. Indigo bunting
of your voice memos. Yellow warbler.
Your bright queer face in the selfies
I'll carry in my purse forever.
Your name the same as my son's—
and the same as my son—chosen
by your single mom. I fall
in love on my phone,
and on my phone,
you leave me.

The Ballad of Swilt Jack

Child of coyote howl &
spilling

        sediment
        down a ravine

Nobody's friend

        friend of nothing

Nothing
but crackled wind
ruddy & bloodshot

        turning a cheek

        A boy
        growing up
        with bulls & bucks

& dark flowers

        A boy who learned early

how meat is made

        Once you know blood
        you carry it
        for life

like that

Forget-me-not
eyes

        rare another human ever
          sees you
        wide open

Squinted up

        on account of the sun
        slanting off

another sorrow

        A mountain rider
        a heart that gets cracked in
        half

by a blade
of grass   An American

a mustang   on a switchback

A stack of horseshoes   in a barn

A communion   of dust
Of grief   Of rust

A river   with its mouth
silted up   a river
with no mouth   to speak of

The Porcupine

Sun slices into the birch's
hollow, spills over a flank
of quills. A splinter of light
across bristles. I whisper
to anything that will listen—
it's a mama guarding her young.

My son is in another state
with his father, a stranger.
And I'm here holding hands
with a man in a forest,
and he's a stranger too.

In the woods, our shadows
show up arrow-sharp.

Non-Monogamy (Ars Poetica)

I have an idea for a poem.
It's just black feathers, forever.
I don't know the ways of ravens,
if they clear their throats
before they caw, what makes them
not crow nor blackbird. A winged thing
can dissolve into a wall of rock,
then become itself again, shrieking.
We don't know why a crevasse
isn't just a crevice, but someone
brought a can of paint into this cave
and sprayed ancient symbols onto slate.
No doubt a man. Just as a man said *making*
art is like giving birth: the thing that turns
your body inside out and your heart
into a raven, scavenging for a scrap of you.
Really it's like being in a room with your son,
then walking out and just letting him speak,
not needing to hear what he says.

HOW UGLY WAS THE BABY

K meets a new baby, days old,
born to two mamas, their neighbors
in the holler. A queer miracle,
the way we're all queer miracles.

Later K's new lover texts them, *how ugly was the baby?*
K replies, *about as ugly as a sunrise*, and to me,
Why do I still date men?

Sometimes we don't want to be here,
on the same earth as my dad's old neighbor in Boca,
the tequila mogul that moved to a golf course
because the ocean was too loud for him.
It kept him up when he was trying to sleep.

I don't want another baby, but when I smelled
the top of V's 10-day-old head, I felt a new sun
rise inside me. An infant isn't the way
a stranger wants it to be. It's the way
our bodies need it to be, to get lodged
inside them. Language itself is made
ugly in the face of it. It keeps you up at night.

This morning, I am writing these two men a letter.
I want them to know my son
has learned every fact about raptors.
Not the dinosaurs. The birds.

Like, do they even know an Andean condor

can soar for a hundred miles on a carpet of air
without once flapping its wings?

Or that a Cooper's Hawk will hold a smaller bird
underwater until it drowns, and eat it after that?
It was too loud.

Or that raptures—I mean, raptors—
eat their whole prayer—
I mean, prey—fur & feather,
bone & tooth?

I want to tell them that yesterday
my son was stopped in his tracks
while putting on his bumblebee rain boots
by our porch robin feeding a worm
to her nestlings. Ugly naked necks
emerging, for the first time made visible
to him. I want to tell them how
my son couldn't speak when he saw this.
He lost six years of vocabulary. He melted
into my body, shrieking in his outside voice—
Oh, Mommy! Oh, oh! Oh!

Forty Names for Catamount
Pownal, Vermont

We think we can capture a creature
by naming it. Long-distance lover.
Partner. *Mountain lion*. Lion Daddy.
Daddy. *American lion*.
Forty names in this language alone.
Dating, but only on FaceTime.
In this language alone. Open. Poly.
Open but not actually poly. Just open.
Puma, cougar, lynx. Why try to love
wildly again? California, California.
Like most things, this animal
has little to do with you,
but like most things it turns
into you, slinking through
the milky darkness of my mind. I stay
locked in its amber eye—Sweetie, Babygirl.
Pretty Thing. Tiny Flower. Just open.
When it's gone into hiding, you start calling
me by my mother-given name. Strange
syllables dropped from your mouth.
Not petals. Just gray stones. Just open.
Stay friends. Growl and tremble.
They say that someone shot the last one,
but people swear they've spotted them—
prowling for scents and pawing at visions.
Painter.   Red tiger.   Mountain screamer.

Daisydog

She's a Goldendoodle
with a dead bunny in her maw.
She doesn't drop it at my feet.
I muscle her jaws apart and reach in.

Later, I brush her out. Clumps fly
as if from dandelions. I wonder
which bird will add this fur
to the weaving of its nest,
nestled in the shadows
of our porch's eaves. I make a wish
on these wisps in the breeze:

Let me love this animal
I named for a flower.
Let me stop wondering how far
down in her belly the wolf
howls, and what had to happen
for it to get quiet.

Petrichor

We trip through the woods, stalking our old addictions

Is this path a loop? And if it isn't, how do we know when
to turn around?

We sing a wetsong, a song in the under

Dark networks, dark reckless, an O-ring necklace

Pink lace between my legs, late sun lacing gold through
deep October trees

My panties flew with you, pink wings, toured Los
Angeles in your pocket

Draped on a gate spike outside The Last Bookstore in
magenta neon light

Light that might say *Girls Girls Girls* beneath a cheaper
moon

Hung on Diana the Huntress in the Huntington library
gardens

Yes, hunting—shot through and strung up by hunger

The small dog of my longing, yelping in bronze, leaping
up beside her
On the steps of the concert hall, my panties singing arias

When you had them, they smelled like me—and now
they smell like you

I lay the lace across my face, my hand casting the spell of
water

Some earth gets wet where you are, a pocketful of rainy
days

Listening to Lana Del Rey in the Woods

I'm counting the spots on this ladybug,
trying to remember my lucky numbers,
whether ladybugs are the lucky ones,
or what the unluckiest bug is. She is
the red I'd kiss Lana's lips with.
The same red as B's Halloween lipstick,
which he'd wear in public every day
in a world that isn't this one.

There is absolutely gold leaf, or tinsel,
or pearlescent confetti on the mushroom
growing out of those shiny bullets
of deer scat, and B isn't here to see it.

Before last weekend, he was a *high-functioning alcoholic*,
a charming hedonistic alchemist who infused his own gin.

Last weekend, he tried to stop drinking for a day
and ended up withdrawal-seizing in a parking lot.

Saint Ladybug. Saint Lana.
Saint Barnabas, you Saint of Second Chances—
bless the EMT who spotted him.

To the ER staff, he was just a regular alcoholic—
slurring in sunglasses, under-reporting
his daily drinks to three different nurses—
not a magical one.

Can I rewind those nurses? How do I re-shimmer him?

Don't forget me, Lana croons into the trees.

B's sleeping on a friend's couch,
and storing his furniture in my basement.

Chickens

The neighbor built a coop,
then filled it with the feathered.
I met him exactly once, when he delivered
misaddressed mail to my door.
I know him by his rooster's
pre-dawn crow, by his ride-along
lawn mower, by watching him
double back across already-cut grass
all summer. I wondered who he did it for,
knowing he lives alone. No—he lives
with chickens. My son asks me,
what would you do if I died? as I crack
a pale supermarket egg into a bowl.
He says *you're my yolk, and I fold around you.*

Dear Emergency

Run—Hide—Fight is our procedure.
This stays with students—inside students—

in a secure location. Practice with students,
beginning with a classroom of students.

Low-stress practice over the intercom,
practicing the word *lockdown*.

The intercom will stop the classroom.
Language includes the word *lockdown*.

We have to practice the word *lockdown*
to get quiet and keep voices off.

Look inside the students. They might tell you
we are leaving, going to space to get quiet.

Another day we will stay inside.
The students will keep their voices off.

November *lockdown*. January *lockdown*.

Any questions?

Watching a Documentary on the Bleaching of Coral Reefs, My Six-Year-Old Says, *I Hope the Reefs Come Back to Life at the End*

When I want to describe what being alive feels like,
I look at his crayon-rendered treasure map,
requiring passage through *The Cav of Lost Sols,*
The Templ of Deth, The Windy Grav Yard.

I hollow out a mountain for the lost soul
of his father, who is alive, but barely.
He disappears and disappears. First-person
shooter games, six-packs of beer, a body
I haven't recognized in years as the body
that was with my body when we made our son.
Sometimes I crawl into the whole
dank mouth of it, squint at the scrawls
on the wall, big-spoon my grief, and sleep.

I build a temple of death, and go to pray in it.
I kneel on a meditation cushion in front of a fire,
getting touched. I make amends for the years
I was casual with my own skull. Death
doesn't scare me, but I fear it. I make offerings
of drugs and cheddar popcorn, knowing
it needs more than me alone.

When I want to describe what being alive feels like,
I dig a hundred holes, throw all my hungers in.
I walk through the cemetery wind,
singing for the fish in Australia.

Owl Hill

I return again, having learned from snails
about time. It's slimy. It's slow. It spirals.

One year ago I thought all kinds of things
would have happened by now. It's quieter

than I remember, because I am quieter,
having learned from water about language:

how it builds, how it takes away.
You can make people disappear with it.

Yesterday I hiked to a stream and spread
a blanket on the earth. For hours I watched

the woods. For hours I didn't think
about my son. I didn't count his eyelashes

in the grass, his freckles on the leaves.
I didn't think about how to mother

this child who loves guns. I studied the earth
in her mothering, how she holds

our endless tragedies, and only lets go
when we explode into stars.

In Nature

We're wrestling when he digs
his knee into the root
of me—familiar tickle—
throb and flare

between my legs,
his naughty smile
pulls a string up
inside me

buries me in dirt
leaves, leaves

the sun, my squinting

we roll around
giggling

Maybe I'll never have another love

When we're done, my son picks
the sticks from my hair

Notes

"To Alanis Morissette, After Reading About Her Postpartum Depression in My Therapist's Waiting Room" borrows lyrics from her songs "You Oughta Know" and "Precious Illusions."

"Old Nipple" and "Mommies" are written in the Duplex form, with tribute and reverence to Jericho Brown.

"Twisties" is after artist Steve Tobin, and takes its title from one of his sculptures.

"Roden Crater" is after James Turrell at the Massachusetts Museum of Contemporary Art.

"The Ballad of Swilt Jack" refers to a fictional "cowboy singer" created by my son.

"Dear Emergency" is an erasure of a letter from my son's principal about emergency preparedness drills at his elementary school.

Acknowledgments

Deep gratitude to the editors of the journals and anthologies where these poems first appeared, some in previous versions:

ballast	"I'm Supposed to be Writing a Nature Poem," "*Spilanthes americana*"
The Boiler	"Opening Track for Sertraline" "Revelations"
Ecobloomspaces	"Owl Hill"
Foundry	"The Excavator"
Fugue	"Reddit"
Gigantic Sequins	"Some Dark Familiar"
Jet Fuel Review	"The Basket"
Lighthouse Weekly	"The Ballad of Swilt Jack"
Memoir Mixtapes	"To Alanis Morissette, After Reading About her Postpartum Depression in My Therapist's Waiting Room"
The Oakland Review	"Uvalde"
Plant-Human Quarterly	"*Pachira aquatica*"
The Raleigh Review	"*Who Makes Milk?*"

Red Noise Collective	"Roden Crater," "Petrichor"
Santa Clara Review	"Old Nipple"
Sixth Finch	"When a Bird Gets Trapped in Your House"
Southern Humanities Review	"Rutland"
SWWIM Every Day	"L'Oeuf Chaud Froid"
Thimble Literary Magazine	"Forty Names for Catamount"
Watershed Review	"Non-Monogamy (Bad Reasons)"
Yemassee	"Non-Monogamy (Lepidoptera)"

Thank you to my family—given and chosen—especially to Lali for supporting me as only a sister can. To my VCFA kin: C. Berry, Susan Audrey Holcomb, Paul Kopp and Bethany Breitland—comrades in the writing life, and first readers of so many of my poems. To Kim Wayman, first reader of so much of my life. To my teachers David Wojahn, Betsy Scholl, and Natasha Sajé. To the Sundog Poetry Center and Matthew Olzmann for plucking my manuscript out of the ether and making my big dream come true. Thank you Dede Cummings and Green Writers Press for the alchemy that transforms the manuscript into the book. To Tomás Q. Morín and Hila Ratzabi for reading and seeing me clearly. To the beautiful, multitudinous humans who have graced my life with inspiration, and who show up in these poems. To Justin Bigos, for opening my poems and my heart to new realms of golden possibility. . .

and to Theo—my one & only—this book begins and ends with you.